The Memoirs of
Ethel Beatrice Vincent

Ethel Gadd in the 1920's

The Memoirs of Ethel Beatrice Vincent
1891-2000

*Published in loving memory
by her three sons*

Crux Press

PUBLISHED BY:
Crux Press
178 Abbeyfield Road, Sheffield S4 7AY
England

© 2008 John and Faith Vincent
All rights reserved

No part of this publication may be reproduced
in any manner written without the permission of
Crux Press.

Editor: John Vincent
Cover and book design: Faith Vincent
at www.faithindesign.com

Front photograph: Gordon, Ethel, Peter & John Vincent 1935
Back Photograph: Ethel with John and Gordon Vincent at
Tonbridge 1930

Photographs from Vincent family archives.

Contents

Early Childhood
1891-1905 6-29

Teens and Twenties
1905-1925 30-39

Six Houses and Three Sons
1925-1935 40-65

Family and Wartime
1935-1945 66-81

Completing the Story

Peter - The Provision Specialist............................82-91
Gordon - Childhood and family life 92-105
John - Later Years...106-117

Ethel and Kate Gadd

Early Childhood
1891 - 1906

※

I was born in 1891 Ethel Beatrice to James Colvin and Kate Amelia Gadd (nee Walker) the elder of their two daughters. My sister Kate May was born 3 1/2 years later; so she does not come into some of my earliest memories, being just "the baby". I was born at Fox Farm, Wadhurst, Sussex, on 8th January 1891.

We were a very happy little family. I adored my parents. They were a fine very young couple and brought us up with great care. They were both of Baptist families at Wadhurst, Sussex but I do not think they knew each other as children as they both lived outside Wadhurst village. My father's home was off the Ticehurst Road and my mother's home right the other way, out on the Lamberhurst Road; both at least 3 miles from the railway station.

My father was the second son of a family of 11, 7 boys and 4 girls. He was born in 1868. Sister Mary was born in 1866 and brother William in 1865. Other children followed – Ephraim, Hannah, Annie, George, Naomi, Charles, Frank and Fred. Two girls died when quite young so that I only knew Auntie Hannah and Auntie Naomi (Nay or Nan as everyone called her). Of these two Auntie Nay came into my life most as she came to live in Tunbridge Wells where my parents had moved to before I can remember.

Mother was the youngest of 3 girls, Elizabeth, Jane and Kate (my mother) and there were 2 sons. Their father was killed when they were quite young. He was an overseer of a stone quarry and the ground gave way. I do not think my mother remembered him as she never spoke of him. Grandma Walker was a beautiful little lady and my sister and I loved her very much.

Grandma Walker with Gordon

    I wonder what is really my earliest memory – I do not know so will write of a few "pictures" in my mind. (I think I must always have had a "mind that takes pictures" as some of the memories are so very clear.) I only remember seeing Grandma Gadd once as she died in her early fifties and I must have been very young. I remember a lovely lady resting back on white pillows, 2 long dark plaits, on a huge 4 poster bed. She was a dear person I am sure. My father always spoke of her with great feeling. She gave me a lovely doll dressed in pale blue and for my baby sister a little pale blue dress. My mother stood with me by the bed with the baby on her arm, so I suppose I must have been about 4 years old.

After she died, Auntie Hannah kept house for Grandpa as there were 2 boys still at school, Frank and Fred. Charles the next youngest came to live with us at Tunbridge Wells. I went to stay there during this time. I was still quite young and Grandpa had made for me a dolls cradle which rocked. It was a lovely old house – I loved it, especially the garden and orchard. There was a very large round table in the middle of the living room and ever such a big fire-place. Grandpa used to sit in a high-back Windsor chair to the side of it and I on a stool at his feet. There were several bedrooms and one was called the "apple room". I slept in a little room off Auntie Hannah's. The garden at the front and side of the house sloped down and at the side it ended in a little brook and this was my father's favourite spot. I was told he planted all sorts of flowers – he loved flowers and a garden. I do not remember any time or house when there were not flowers around.

Some years ago, maybe in 1972 or 1973, David (my husband) and I were in Sussex for some weeks and we went to Wadhurst as I wanted to find the house if possible. We turned off the main road past the Strict Baptist Chapel which looked as if it were still being used, and on down the lanes between high hedges and eventually came to "Buttons" but I could not remember it all. I think the roads were wider, the banks at the sides of the road more tidy and trim and this put me out a little. (When I stayed there the boys, my uncles really, used to find mauve and white violets for me to take in to Auntie Hannah.)

There was a seat under a tree at the bend of the road so we sat down and a youngish man, about 40 perhaps, came and sat with us and, as is the custom in the country, passed the time of day with us. I told him I was a "Gadd" and had hoped to find their home. He smiled and said, "There it is, over on the corner". He was right, it was in beautiful condition, not really altered very much, an outside porch had been built on, and what was once the back door was now the front I presume. The steep path leading up to the house was now made into 2 or 3 steps at a time, still a small gate, garden each side and just a little way down the road the little bridge that went over the brook. The orchard was gone, it was now a field and the garden at the side was gone and a garage built there

James Colvin Gadd

to match the house. Upstairs it looked the same with its small paned windows and yes, there was the room I had slept in all those years ago. I tried to take a snap but the light was fading but I did stand by the little gate and on the bridge and looked down on what was, a long time ago, a little piece of beauty which my father had loved and tended.

I did not go to stay at Buttons after I started school. I believe when Auntie Hannah married the house was given up and Grandpa went to live with her. Frank and Fred both came in time to live with us at Tunbridge Wells, each of them, including Charles, found work in Tunbridge Wells. Eventually Charles married and went with his wife and her family to Canada. Frank and Fred both went to America and Auntie Nay used to write to them all but I do not think my father did very often.

Now I must write a little of my school days and home life. Later I will write about dear Grandma Walker (Mamma's mother), whom we both loved very much. As I have already written, we were a Baptist family (nonconformist) and at that time the line between Church of England and ourselves was very wide and whenever it was possible parents sent their children to private day schools. So at 5, I went to school in a house, Mrs Brand's, and her 2 daughters were our teachers. I think they must have taught us very well because when I started at the Grosvenor School at 7 I went straight into Standard 2. The Grosvenor Schools were run by a Board of all non-conformist people, nothing to do with the C of E or the Government. They did not take children under 7, hence my 2 years at the "baby school". Our teachers were good and I believe the school had quite a reputation in Tunbridge Wells. I was very happy there, I liked lessons and my teachers.

The education was good – two senior teachers and two younger ones, also a man, Mr Hobble, for French. He also took one of the boys' classes. We girls and boys did not learn together. We had great respect for our teachers. They were very kind. But the teachers had respect for us. There was never any corporal punishment. There was the head teacher, Miss Saxby, and Miss Hasley, and Miss Hanimond who taught maths. We had lead pencils and slates, and then pencils and paper. The great day of our year was about 10 days before Christmas when we had our "Breaking Up Concert" with songs, drills, little plays mostly in costume, and one year a rather special display of Japanese kimonos and sunshades, I remember it so well. This concert was given in the Town Hall and was by invitation, mostly "parents only" (except for a lot of Chapel people who I gather were those really responsible for the school and its upkeep. We did pay a weekly fee but I cannot think that covered the cost.

Towards the end of my school days the Technical Institute was opened and, for a small fee, we could go twice a week (if you were in Class X7) for cookery and one other subject we could choose. I was fond of writing and figures so I went to the Book-Keeping and Shorthand Class and enjoyed it very much. The schools were for boys and girls but we were not together, their entrance was in another road really and they had a large playground but we had our entrance space and large lobby. We were not allowed to speak to the boys. We were expected to go straight home after school, little groups of girls wandering along together on the pavements - I wonder why the pavements as there were no motor cars, only horse-drawn carts etc, mostly tradesmen.

Going shopping was not the great thing as it seems to be today. The baker, milk (twice a day), butcher, greengrocer all came for orders and delivered as required and in the Autumn at the end of the day the fishman would go along calling "Fresh herrings" etc. They would have been caught that same morning no doubt at Hastings and sent up by rail. Early morning the "Hot rolls" man would call as he went along (they were lovely – I would like one right now as I write) and late afternoon the "Muffins and Crumpets" call. They carried their large wooden trays on their heads covered with a white cloth and a green baize cover. In the Winter if there was a heavy fall of snow it would be around for weeks, the horse-drawn plough just went down the middle of the road and snow piled up each side. The pavements were left more or less to the people in the houses and oh! how slippery it used to be. Mamma used to put old socks over our shoes to keep us from falling. High boots were fashionable (no Wellingtons), laced up the front but a nuisance as we had to have slippers at school for lesson time.

    Our home was not far from the school, a small house with a tiny garden which was full of flowers in the Summer (Daddy and Mamma loved flowers), window boxes at the windows. Dad made them I expect – they had pieces of tree bark put along the front and the blue and white Lobelia used to trail over, also a little yellow flower called "Musk". There was a little tiny beach stone path – whenever we went to the sea (Sunday school outings etc) we always took back some tiny beach stones for Daddy. He was always doing things in the house. He fixed bells at the front and back door, charged (I know not how) from some liquid in jars on a shelf in the scullery. We felt very important over this. Our scullery today would be called the kitchen, as it was where the cooking etc was done. We had gas lighting (mantles) and Mother had a gas cooker. There was a large dresser for all the crockery and a large table for baking and ironing and a brick-built boiler in the corner for boiling the laundry. This needed a real coal fire for heating, and washing day was quite a task. We did not use the table for meals, as these we always ate in the living room.

There were gas lights in the streets, and May and I used to watch for the "lamp lighter" to come along with his long pole, it had a hook on the end which fitted round the little tap and the light came on. On Saturdays there were stalls all along the main street Calverley Road, and in the Winter they were lit by swinging oil lamps. Mother never went shopping there but sometimes Dad would take us for a walk and we would come that way home. The only thing I ever remember Dad buying was fresh watercress or a bunch of early wallflowers. He liked football and used to go sometimes to watch the local team.

There is a beautiful Common at Tunbridge Wells. The road that ran along the top was called Mt Ephrium. It was all large houses (mostly hotels) with gardens and flowering trees and was a favourite walk for everyone. On Sundays, after

Kate Amelia Gadd

Church it was like the Prom of a seaside resort, all the fashion of the day, no cars and very few carriages, even wealthy people seldom used them on Sundays in the towns. I think everyone looked upon Sunday as a "day of rest" which included, as far as possible, servants as well. On Sunday afternoons the Salvation Army held an open air meeting on the Common. They had quite a large following as did most of the Churches and Chapels; and a very fine band. Mum and Dad used to meet us after Sunday School and we would walk along together. There are hills and sand in places on the Common but children did not run and make a noise very much on Sundays, it was just not done. The sunshine, lovely music and everyone in pretty summer dresses (and hats) and to be out with our parents leaves a very beautiful memory.

In the Winter we went straight home, most Sundays with one or more friends to tea, Sunday tea was always very special to us. Mother was a good cook and there were always 2 or 3 different cakes, bread and butter (cut thin and laid on plates) home-made jam (Mother made a lot of jam and we never had any bought jam), celery, lettuce and watercress. I do not remember tomatoes so perhaps we in England had not discovered them at that time. We had an harmonium in the living room and Mother used to play a little and we used to sing hymns. Later, when it was decided I should learn to play the piano it was sold and a piano bought. This I loved as it had a lovely red silk front behind fretwork, beautiful wood. Years later we had a more modern one but I never liked it as much as the old one. We kept it for years and used it and I think my cousin Lily had it when Mother got rid of many things after Daddy died just after I married.

We had a happy childhood, enough toys, home made and otherwise, usually we had a cat which we all loved. I remember once when it was a kitten, May dressed it in doll's clothes and put it in the dolls' pram. To her joy it went to sleep and we left the pram just outside. Later we saw it running up the garden (or trying to), it looked so funny. Later when asked why she loved the kitten so much more than playing with dolls she said "it's alive and warm and cuddly" (how true). She was a very pretty child, everyone loved her. I am afraid I often felt it was unfair that I had to wear glasses (which I had at about 5 1/2 years old). They were not fashionable then and boys in the street would call out "four eyes" etc. I thought my glasses made people dislike me, such are the "hurts" of a child.

I first had piano lessons when I was about 9 years old. I loved playing and it was no trouble to me to practice for an hour each day. I did not like my first teacher because she pulled my hair if I did not keep my eyes on the music but later I went to Miss Thorpe and she was very different. Sometimes she came to our house to give me my lesson and stayed to tea and she taught me to sing and played for me. There was no radio or television then to get in the way of doing something nice in the home.

Auntie Nay often came to see us. We loved her, she always looked so nice and she used to make her own hats, also for Mother and we two girls. She taught me to knit and do embroidery and later after she married, she would sometimes meet me from school on Friday and take me home with her for the night. I had to go back home on Saturday ready for Sunday School at 10 o'clock, Chapel at 11 o'clock, Sunday School at 2.30 and (when we were older) Evening Service at 6.30. We were always quite happy with our Sundays as I have already written. It meant a walk with our parents and friends to tea. Most people went to Church or Chapel and there was always a good congregation.

I want to write about holidays when we were very young. Dad had a brother George who lived at Eastbourne and they had 2 sons about our age and we often went to see them for a day or two. Eastbourne is still a favourite place of mine, very prim and proper with its perfect flowerbeds and lovely promenade and at the end, Beachy Head. We had some lovely walks up there. The two families and May and I spent some happy holidays there in later years. George and his family went to Australia while I was still at school. There must be quite a few "Gadds" scattered around what used to be the Colonies.

Now for our real holidays, this means "Wadhurst", the country, only perhaps about 10 to 15 miles from home, but to us, another world. Tunbridge Wells at this time was really only a county town of about 30,000 people and was surrounded on all sided by open countryside. Whenever we had an odd day off from school Mother took us to see Grandma Walker (her mother). She lived at Pell Green (Wadhurst) in a dear little house with a beautiful red rose tree in the front garden. It really was a tree! I have never seen anything like it since. There was a table full of flowers in the front of the living room window, with geraniums of all colours, fuschias etc. There was a large Chesterfield in the room covered in a light cover and 2 very hard bolster-like cushions, one at each end and, always waiting for us, was a large rag doll, clothes and bonnet (which we took off and on) and a lovely drink of lemonade. This was served in a very large earthenware jar with a cork. It was very special. Sometimes we stayed a few days and Daddy would come on the Saturday and we all went back together on Sunday evening. The railway station was at the bottom of a hill and as we walked down we would be facing the sunset. This enchanted me and I remember thinking that must be "Heaven" as it was so beautiful. Sunsets are and always have been a great glory to me.

In the morning we walked up the hills with grassy banks each side, primroses and, if you were lucky, violets in the spring, and wild roses in summer. I used to wonder how people remembered where they had "put their money". I knew (at that time) no other "bank" than those by the roadside! At the back of Grandma's house was a large piece of ground and quite a lot of chickens lived there in coops about the size of tea chests . The baby chicks could go in and out between the laths but the Mother hen could only put her head through and cluck. When the chicks were a little older she was allowed out with them and how lovely they looked hovering around her.

I cannot remember Grandma making bread. A baker with a horse-drawn cart came round, but not every day. She did a lot of baking, lovely pastry and cakes – there were always cakes and pies, as the different fruits came along, and jam tarts, large and small. Our "special" pudding was a "Well Pudding". I think it must have been a suet crust which lined the basin and in the middle, brown sugar and sultanas (or raisins as they were called then), which made a lovely syrup but quite different from bought golden syrup. Pork was used a lot. I think the butcher only came round once a week. Pork was kept in an earthenware sink-like vessel in the pantry where it was kept in a 'brine'. Many people kept pigs but those who didn't bought from others, either a whole pig or half or cut up and pickled in the brine. (These mysteries, I learned as I grew older.)

When Grandma went to Chapel she would wear a long black dress, a black cape and bonnet, with some white at the neck and sleeves and around her face in the bonnet. To me she looked lovely. In those far off days it was not unusual for a widow to keep to black for the remainder of her life. We had a nice photograph of her in the album which used to be on the table in our sitting room. I wonder what happened to that lovely old album with its clasp to fasten it. Grandma died when I was about 13.

Sundays were spent between home and the Baptist

Chapel. Both my parents were Baptists. It was a busy day on Sunday but a very loveable one. We went to Sunday School at about 10 o'clock in the morning. Years later, I could play the piano well enough to play for the hymns. Then after Sunday School we went upstairs to church. I do not remember when Dr Mountain first came as the Minister. His doctorate came from America, and he started the building of the Sunday School, which was used as a church while the church was being built over it. The road was on a hill.

We lived in Victoria Road in a row of houses. My daddy was the first person to install a bell to the front door, and, if I remember it rightly, the battery for the bell was in the scullery, which we would call the kitchen. In the corner in the scullery was a built copper with a brick surround, which had to be made up in the usual way each night. Mother did all the washing at the sink and dropped it into a large zinc bath of blue water. We had a mangle, which took the water out, which was used again later to flatten clothes. Almost everything was ironed. The clothes dried in the yard and garden.

The yard and garden were outside the back door. There was a wire flower holder on the wall, with flowers in the top, cooking things in the cupboard. She did all the baking in the scullery. In the kitchen, there was a cupboard for food, including all the jams which were made.

There was also another cupboard where we had coal. We did not store food. We did not preserve food, except jams. The floor was tiles or bricks in both the kitchen and scullery. Everything which had to be kept for a day or two was placed on the brick floor and covered.

I've just remembered. In the kitchen mother had a very nice sewing machine, which mother used a lot, as she made all our clothes. Later, I think, she had a harmonium, which she could play sufficiently well for us to sing.

The kitchen was also the living room. There was also a front room, the sitting room, which later had a piano in it. The dear lady who taught me to play the piano used to pull my hair if I made a mistake. Later I went to Prospect road for lessons.

I was eight when the new century started, but I do not remember anything special. I remember that we had black arm bands and bow when Queen Victoria died in 1901.

London was a long way from Tunbridge Wells, and it was a different world. It was only 30 miles, but it was a long way. There were horse buses, and there were trains. We went by train to see Grandma in Wadhurst and the fare was 5d. Grandma lived at Wadhurst where I was born, and so did Daddy's people. Mummy used to take us for a day to Grandma's.

On special occasions and birthdays we always had a cake. My birthday was just two weeks after Christmas, and my birthday party was the return party for all the children whose parties we had been to in the Christmas period. We had lots of children, with blancmanges and jellies, but no ice cream, also a glass with cut celery in it, which the parents who called for the children, would eat with cheese and biscuits. They were mostly Chapel people and they used to sing together. We played games like musical chairs.

Most of mother's shopping was done near to home. Practically everything was bought in the local shops.

After a time at Victoria Road, Daddy was very ill. There was nothing to hide, more to admire. Mother decided that she could not possibly carry on a home with an invalid for a husband. So she looked for a larger house where she could take lodgers.

The house was in Garden road, a large stone built house, with three storeys and a long garden with fruit trees, also a front garden and lawn with a Monkey tree. I must have been around 10-12, as I was still at school. Eva and I became great friends at this time, and we have remained friends for nearly a hundred years.

Daddy had rheumatic fever and then he got blood poisoning, which was caused by inspecting drains. He was headman for a builder. They paid us some money but there was no money coming in. But my mother borrowed some money from her sister – not very much, but enough to furnish one floor of the house, and with our own furniture we furnished the other floors. She was able to carry on that way.

So from me being 10 or 12, Mother had people as paying guests. There were 4, 5 or 6 steps to the front door. We used the breakfast room, but evening meals were served in the front room. Daddy went back to light work after a while, but he never really got better.

    Mother bought a lovely mahogany sideboard at a sale. It was very large, too large for an ordinary house, and it was lost in our breakfast room, as the rooms were very large. I used to sit at the table and she would say 'Change your place at the table as I cannot have you looking at yourself in the mirror.'

Ethel Beatrice Gadd in the 20's

Teens and Twenties
1905 - 1925

I went into the Choir at about 14, as did my special friend, Eva Goddard . She and I have never really lost touch with each other over the years. We both went to a Choral Society at about 17 or so, we could both play the piano and loved music so were accepted after a voice test. We loved it as it was wonderful to be a tiny part in such great things as The Messiah, Elijah, Bach's Passion and many other great works. We wore long cream dresses for the "Great Night", the contraltos wore black, also all the male singers, very much as one sees them today in the "Male Voice Choirs".

Those were happy days in our singing world. We both loved music and often went together in the evenings in Summer to listen to the Military Bands who played either on the Pantiles or in The Grove (a lovely open space of trees and flower beds with swings etc for children at one end). Tunbridge Wells at that time was quite an important Spa town and there was a different band every week during the Summer. If it was wet they played in the Pump Rood at the far end of the Pantiles and when under cover it was usually string instruments and there were always at least 2 solo singers. How we enjoyed those evenings, a deck chair for 6 pence or a small fold up for 3 pence. Not everyone sat down, there was a promenade to and from on the Pantiles and walks all around amongst the flowerbeds in the Grove. It was in this Pump Room that our Choral Society gave the concerts except when we were doing something for charity when it would be given in a Church. From a postcard I received in 1982 the Pantiles looks very much as I remember it but the Pump Room has gone and is now a superstore. Oh! If only those people who shop there knew all the lovely music they are walking on.

When I left school at 14, I went into business. The superintendent minister spoke for me at Williamsons Limited,

Ethel with her father James 1920

which was a private firm not far from home. I did office work. I was hot stuff for writing. When I watch Reuben my great-grandson, I often think of how I used to enjoy writing. There was not a lot of money at the shop. It was very high class trade. The majority of the customers had a monthly account. Whatever they or the servants bought and signed for would be entered into the book. Then, at the end of the month – my job – the bills were sent out in an envelope. Williamsons sold provisions, wines, spirits, fruit, grapes, groceries, lovely canisters of tea and coffee, beautiful vases of different sizes for the window dressing. It was a corner shop so there were lots of windows. I worked 6 days a week, from 8 or 9 am until 6 or 7pm in the evening.

I stayed 4 or 5 years at Williamsons. The house in Garden Road came on the market, to be sold, but mother did not feel she could take on the responsibility. Daddy was ill again as well as May. At the top of the stairs, May had the study as a bedroom, and they moved her up to the second floor so that she was nearer to them. May had rheumatic fever and St Vitus Dance. The doctor recommended Great Ormond Street Hospital in London. After a little time we were able to get May there, and she was there for six months. They cured her of St Vitus Dance, and she had grown very tall when she came back home and her hair was cut short. And she was Lovely.

After Garden Road, daddy and mummy moved to 6 Dunston Road, Tunbridge Wells. It was not quite such a big house as Garden Road. Mummy carried on letting. We had a lovely garden there. Daddy was better, and he made it very beautiful. Down the bottom of the garden were some apple trees, and under the apple trees was a hammock where

Kate May Leckie and daughter

May and I used to rest, especially on half days, when she finished at 2 o'clock. And if she wanted the hammock, and I was on it, she just turned it over and I fell out. I must have been around 18 or 19.

Mummy had a girl, Helen, from chapel, who worked as a servant for us. She adored mother. I think she thought my mother walked on gold. Helen did everything in the house. She did not sleep in, or eat with us, as she had an invalid father, and would leave at dusk. No-one else ever entered moth-

Ethel Gadd

er's kitchen. She did all the cooking. She did not teach me to cook. I went to business. And it was important that I should be immaculate. She would look at my hands to make sure they were kept nice. May was very ill and did not work. When she got better she stayed home and helped mummy. She never went to business or worked.

David Vincent

    May got married, and went to New Zealand. After all she had been through, she married someone from Australia. There was no chance that she would ever come back. People at our station at that time didn't expect to come back. Daddy's cousin, who lived at Eastbourne, had two sons about our age, who went to Australia but never came back. It was a great shock, when she went and it was very sad, as she was never very strong, and suffered with her heart. Mother knew she would never come back, and she didn't.

During my twenties and early thirties, we had a very homely existence. Easter and Whitsuntide Mondays were a general holiday when there were stalls on the Tunbridge Wells common. Daddy took us to them.

Daddy died aged 56 in 1924. My mother died aged 63 in 1934. I did not have either of them for a long time.

In my twenties I got a job in Sainsbury's, in Tunbridge Wells. I eventually became the Head Book Keeper. In 1923, David came to Tunbridge Wells, where I was working at Sainsbury's. He came as a relief manager, but it was a year or two later where we really got to know each other.

David and his side car

St Mary's Church, Edenbridge April 5th 1926

Six Houses and Three Sons
1925-1935

※

After leaving school, having taken bookkeeping and shorthand lessons at school, I obtained a post in an office and continued employed until my marriage to David Vincent. David and I were married on April 5th, 1926, at St Mary's Church, Edenbridge, Kent. It was a beautiful day. David was a church bell ringer, and the ringers of the church rang perfectly for us.

On May 8th, my dear father died. We lived at Kettering, Northamptonshire, where David was employed as manager with Thoroughgood, a retail provisions firm. This was a nice house and garden with a small garage for our motorbike and sidecar.

    Shortly after our marriage, David was made Inspector and had to supervise their shops up and down the country, from 1926 to 1936. We had 6 homes and 3 sons: Gordon George, September 2nd 1927, John James, December 29th 1929 and Peter David, April 17th 1933.

The six houses were:
Apr 1926	The Broadway, Kettering
Feb 1927	Gordon Road, West Bridgeford, Nottingham
Oct 1929	Roker, Sunderland
Dec 1931	76 Victoria Road, Urmston
Apr 1933	Tynholme, Haxby, York
Feb 1935	York House, Queens Road, Hale, Cheshire

Then in June 1936 to 6 Stanway Drive, Hale, Cheshire (A home of our own at last)

    First, in February 1927, we moved to 111 Gordon Road, West Bridgeford, Nottingham, in very thick snow. Mother and I had to walk a long way from the bus on a main road. At Easter 1927, Grandpa Vincent came to be with us until August.

David with Gordon 1929

On September 2nd Gordon George was born, at the end of a beautiful day, our first son, he was all we desired, a beautiful child. My Mother was with us at his birth, and off and on for short periods. The garden, which was a "tip" when we moved in (it was a new house) was beautiful. We even had a little lawn at the back, and a wonderful vegetable garden, with a front garden full of flowers.

In September 1928 we had two lovely weeks at a Boarding House in Skegness with our lovely baby. We went in the motorbike and side car. Everyone loved our little son. Shortly after, Grandpa Vincent came back to live with us and stayed until October 1929. We sold the motorbike and bought a little Morris Coupé. It was good for David for bell ringing trips but Gordon did not like it. Baby and I had to go in the back seats which had no top cover, so we were not able to use it very much as a family.

David was away a lot. He was now an inspector, as the firm was now expanding (Thoroughgood) and he had much to do with the fore-opening of new shops. Grandpa Vincent was a nice little gentleman to have around. He was never impatient with Gordon, who was a good child and very fond of him. He with me, missed David when he did not come home in the evenings.

In Summer 1929, my Mother married David Neate and they came to live at Keyworth, a village not far from West Bridgeford. I think she just could not bear life without her home. She was not used to being just a housekeeper in someone else's house. She hadn't a lot of money and was not

David and Gordon at Skegness 1929

old enough for a widow's pension. They were red letter days when she came to see us for a day. She adored Gordon, and spoilt him if she could. She bought him a wooden horse for his first birthday; he loved it. He was already walking when he was at Skegness. We used to go round and round the garden, and we spent quite a lot of time on our little lawn.

David took Grandpa Vincent back to London in August (to Croydon), as we were expecting to move to Sunderland. As soon as he could David found a house for us, which was not easy, as he was only able to look around in the evenings. It was sad to leave West Bridgeford. David had done so much to the garden (and Grandpa Vincent as far as he was able). We had put a lot of work into that little house. It was a long way to go away from Mother, she was not very happy, and it must have been a wrench to her.

We moved in October into a nice little end house (but oh so cold), no garden to speak of, but it had a garage which was a help. David could not use the car very much though as his journeys were too long and complicated. David had the house decorated right through before we moved, and we settled in very well, but it was very lonely. I could not go out very much but fortunately a person over the road was willing to come in the mornings, and took Gordon out sometimes. Her daughter, Evelyn, about 8, used to come and play with him, which helped a lot. We had a quiet, happy Christmas. Daddy was home, so all was well.

John arrived (after I had made 24 mince pies in the morning) safely on 29th December 1929 at Roker, Sunderland. A very wintery day, lots of snow everywhere only the main roads were useable. Both the doctor and the nurse had to

Ethel and Gordon George Vincent 1928

walk quite a distance, but I had a dear friend with me, she was splendid and a great comfort. We had another dear little son.

    A day or two later, David was sent to Hull, another shop to arrange etc etc. He was away three weeks, neither baby nor I were very well, but the nurse was wonderful. Eventually Daddy was home with us again, much to Gordon's delight and mine.

But he was never at home for many weeks without being sent somewhere. Things were not easy for him as he was really Manager of the Fawcett Street shop, in Sunderland. Reliable staff was always difficult. As soon as I was able to go out I went to Church in Roker to say "thank you" for our second little son as I had done at West Bridgeford after Gordon was born.

Mother came to us for a little holiday in the summer, which was lovely for us all. Her husband was at Matlock having treatment which was his usual habit, but I really do not know what for, he was a retired school master, and much respected in Keyworth where they lived. He was also 'church' (not chapel as Mother was). Grandpa Vincent never came to live with us at Roker. It was cold from the sea, and he had a troubled chest. We all went to Keyworth for David's holiday (2 weeks). We had a week there and then went on to Croydon and stayed with Alice and Jim, at least the little boys and I. David went to Suffolk and he took Grandpa Vincent with him, ringing peals etc.

We all had a shock when they returned, as they

David, John and Gordon at Whitley Bay June 1930

brought a Mr Gray back with them who had invited himself (more or less) and intended having a holiday with us for 2 weeks (he was an old railway employee and could travel at reduced fares around the country so there was no problem for him going back). The weather was good and he was out walking quite a lot. But I think he imagined David's time was his own, and was disappointed not to be taken out in the car a lot. It was impossible for me to do much for him with 2 little lads around and meals to prepare (when Daddy was at the shop he usually came home to midday dinner the first 4 days of the week).

John was quite a different baby to Gordon, who was very fair and chubby. John was very slight, a lot of dark hair but the same blue eyes (we all have blue eyes). The first few months were not easy for the little one, it was a very severe winter and he was "chesty" and looked so frail at times. David was away a lot and as we had only moved to Sunderland from Nottingham in October, I had few friends. It was a lonely time but the summer came at last, though I do not remember ever walking along by the sea pushing the pram when the wind was not blowing.

Gordon loved the baby and they were always happy together. He was also a great comfort to me, though only 2¼ he was quite "grown up for his age". We had a Morris Coupé and our red letter days were when Daddy had some time off and we could go out together. Once or twice we went to North Shields or Redcar and just stayed by the sea if the weather was good.

We decided to "lay up" the car for the winter but to take a run to Darlington on the last Sunday in September

Ethel, Gordon and John at Tonbridge July 1930

1930 to see some friends. We had a very enjoyable time with them, leaving about 4.30. We were nearing Sunderland on a very busy wide road and had just passed the AA patrol when a fast sports car crashed into ours turning it over onto the grass verge. The front and windscreen were smashed, one wheel was off, David's hands were cut but the children were unhurt. It was a miracle; baby John was asleep in my arms, Gordon sitting on a hassock with his head against me, half asleep. Within seconds, the AA were with us, I handed up my precious children and was then helped to scramble out myself. Even after all these years I can still see the lights of cars and people all around, as the traffic was at a standstill both ways. A doctor appeared from a car, and as he was also returning home to Sunderland it was he that kindly took us all home. I cannot remember much about that evening after the crash. I think both David and I were rather badly shocked. I have never wanted to drive a car, although I must have travelled many miles since then. We did not buy another car until 1938; our poor Morris was valued at £5 when picked up, but our two little sons were safe. (A Morris Coupé has only the front seats under cover which meant we were all together in the front of the car)

    Summer 1931 was better and I was able to take the boys out much more. Mother came to stay with us which was nice as David was away more than ever. Late summer, the firm suggested another move, this time into the Manchester area, and after much coming and going, David eventually found us a little house in Urmston. I began to get some packing up done, ready for another move, with the "help" of two small boys. This eventually took place on 2nd December 1931, Johnny was nearly 2. It was another bitterly cold snowy day. The furniture left on December 1st, the little ones and I stayed the night with my friend who came with us to the station in the

Gordon and John in Sunderland 1931

morning. So began our journey to our next home.

    The boys were very good but it was a long way for them and as we neared Manchester, Johnny fell asleep so that when we arrived I had a sleeping child in my arms, 2 cases and a little lad of 4½ , and I did not know the city, only that I had to get a bus to Urmston. A gentleman helped me, took the cases and Gordon's hand, led us out of the station, to the bus station and helped us aboard. To this day my very deep thanks go out to all who kindly help old people and mothers and children (and the little one slept on through it all). It was a long bus ride and the conductor had been told to tell me when we reached the road I wanted, and where David was to meet us. But he forgot and we eventually were the only ones left, then he suddenly remembered and was full of apologies. Fortunately we were not very far from Flixton, the end of the journey and the turn around for the bus. You can imagine the surprise on David's face when the bus stopped on the opposite side of the road. We had, at last, arrived.

    The snow was very deep and we seemed to be the only people out of doors but when we reached the house there was a lovely fire and the welcome smell of a meal cooking. David had prepared it for us. He had been in Manchester in digs and had taken some of his clothes there each time he had been home, but apart from that we only had the 2 cases I had brought, mostly our nightwear etc. The furniture had not arrived but about an hour later some young people from a few

David, John and Gordon on beach 1935

doors down the road came to ask if we needed blankets etc. as they had not seen the removals van.

    They brought us large square cushions and blankets and we made up a bed on the floor fitting them close together. We washed and put on the boys all the jerseys on top of their sleeping suits and put them down to sleep in the middle (which did not take long). David lay on one side and I on the other, David kept getting up to keep the fire going, but, in between we slept, two very thankful people warm and safe together.

About 10 o'clock the van arrived. The two men were perished as they had spent the night on the moors, fog and snow making it impossible to keep going. David had stocked up the larder and we soon had hot drinks and soup for them. They stayed in Urmston for the next night after helping David to put up beds. They did a good job and we were very grateful. David had a few days off to help me get settled in, then back to work, and away to different shops as they were all preparing for Christmas. Regarding Christmas, it was much more difficult in those days, no frozen turkeys or other foods, and the last 2 or 3 weeks were very busy (and worrying) especially if the weather turned mild.

David had to leave us the next day for London. He was no longer a manager of one shop but inspector of a number, so was away a lot, often leaving about 6 o'clock Monday morning, back home on Wednesday and away again until Saturday or Sunday. Those 3 weeks before Christmas were busy. All sorts of things happened. I had a burst pipe, which caused a lot of trouble and baby John had a bad chest. The lady next door got a plumber for me, then a doctor for John. We got through and had a long happy Christmas with Daddy home. Really we were nearer Flixton than Urmston. Flixton Church had a good band of singers, so Daddy soon fitted in happily with the very little spare time he had.

Urmston was a cosy little home. No 76 was at the end of the road which was a cul-de-sac, a safe run for the boys on Gordon's tricycle with John standing on the back. They made friends with a little girl who lived opposite called Diane and spent many happy hours together in our little garden. The tricycle was not "all colours" as those of today but a miniature of a real grown up type as were still used in the country at that time. They were happy children and John missed Gordon very much when in September 1932 he started school. They were always good friends playing together, I was sad too. In those days there were no nursery schools and even 5 years old seemed too young, but they were well taught and most mothers had done quite a lot to prepare their children for class work.

Soon after Christmas, Grandpa Vincent came back to live with us, and in the summer of 1932 Mr Gray came again. Mother also came for a few days. In July, we booked Board at

Prestatyn for Grandpa, the boys and I and Daddy, when he could manage a day or two with us. The weather was good. We were quite near the beach, just right for the lads. Grandpa could walk there. I had a photo taken of the boys and one of Grandpa, a copy of which we sent to all the family.

There was not much garden for Grandpa Vincent to look after, but he trotted around. He was then about 85, fairly well, but his chest bothered him and he was very ill just after Christmas. When he was well enough, on March 2nd I think, we got him into a private home that we found through the doctor. Mother came a week or so later.

Just after Christmas (1932) Gordon had chicken pox and John took it. He was very poorly for some weeks and it spoilt my effort to prepare him for the arrival of our 3rd child Peter, who was born on April 17th 1933, a lovely baby, no trouble, but John did not approve of someone taking his place. He would often say "put the baby down mummy" but he eventually got used to the little one, and, as always Gordon was a great help. He loved the baby and eventually brought Johnny round.

Ethel with baby Peter, Gordon and John 1933

    Some weeks before, I had been fortunate in finding a dear person about my own age, a widow with one girl, Joyce, age about 10. She lived with 2 unmarried sisters, school teachers, and was glad to earn a little money to help the small pension she had. She was just splendid to me and the children. She came each day until Joyce came home from school. The boys called her Auntie. I was glad to have her when Mother went back home. That was the last time Mother came to stay with us.

Our next move in April 1933 was to Haxby, near York, a nice little house. David, as usual, got busy with the garden, laid a lawn down and trimmed all the hedges and shrubs. I liked Tyneholm as it was called. It was lovely and open and safe for the boys, as it was not a through road, but an avenue off the main road.

In September 1933 we booked a Chalet at Tynymorfa, Prestatyn for 2 weeks. David hired a car and driver to take us and all the "bits and pieces". Peter was then nearly 5 months old, a lovely baby. I had no trouble; Daddy was with us and he and the boys spent a lot of time on the sands and in the sea. It was a happy holiday. (Grandpa Vincent had gone back to Croydon to live with Alice, eldest daughter of the family.) Mother was far from well but I could not get away to stay with her with my little family to care for.

At Christmas David brought the lads new tricycles. John was supposed to have a tricycle but they came home with 2 wheels. David said Johnny said "I want a 2 wheeler", so that was that. Unfortunately, he came a "cropper" just down the road, and, as the road was not properly made up, he was badly shaken and bruised. A gentleman saw him come off and brought him home and helped me to bathe and comfort him. But it did not deter him from riding his "two wheeler".

We were fortunate in getting Gordon into the school at Earswick (the Rowntree Model Village), it was just a bus ride along the road to York. But he was not there many weeks before he was taken ill with a deep severe attack of tonsillitis. The doctor came every day for a week or so, he was most kind to us. He came twice one day and brought a colleague. There was a lot of diphtheria that year, it was a very anxious time. The weather in summer 1934 was wearily hot. I slept on the landing several nights to be near Gordon, he was so ill. There did not seem a breath of air in spite of all the windows open. Daddy had to "carry on" as usual so it was lonely and very sad at times for me. But Gordon eventually began to get better. It was hard for David to have to leave us, but there was no "let up" in his work.

In 1934 I went to Nottingham to see my Mother twice during the Summer, whenever Daddy had a day off. It was a difficult journey by trams and buses. I took the baby with me and David looked after the boys. But in the Autumn, mother was much worse. Our dear good friends Ernest and Marjorie Bromley, in Scunthorpe, had the lads for 2 weeks but this in the end was 4 weeks, as Mother died on October 26th 1934. David joined me at Keyworth and we decided to take Mother's coffin back to Wadhurst where my Daddy was buried. It was their home village, and they were together again, the coffin rested in a chapel for one night at Tunbridge Wells and we went on to Wadhurst the next day, our Minister with us after a service in the Chapel of St Johns Church, Baptist. (now a United Reformed Church)

We had the baby Peter with us. He was no trouble and was much admired, he looked lovely in a little velvet light cream coat and leggings. It was the only time the relations and friends saw any of our children. It was many years later when David and I were able to go touring that way. We had no car at this time, so I could only bring linen etc from Keyworth. I had to leave the furniture, and other treasures like vases. It was a sad ending and often I remember things or wonder what happened to them. Mother had a sale before she left Tunbridge Wells and came to West Bridgeford, only keeping what she needed, so it is likely things I lost sight of were sold.

    After a few days we returned home to Haxby (York). Our dear friend Marjorie was on the platform with our 2 boys; it was a wonderful reunion. We settled down and Gordon went back to school. Christmas came but we did not see much of Daddy. I could shop quite well in the village, when walking around with the baby and Johnny's lovely pram, back lined in white leather. Auntie Finlayson (our dear friend of Urmston days) saw it advertised and went to see it and brought it for us. I somehow managed to get all the little presents, tree etc for Christmas. Each time Daddy came home he seemed to have found something for them. Christmas Eve we were waiting for him but the children had to go to bed and it was between 1 and 2 o'clock before he arrived (back from York). His train had been held up at some wayside halt and it was 4 o'clock before we got to bed. He had brought a set of fairy lights for the tree and they were not easy to fix, but he managed. It was worth doing, the boys were delighted.

    It was a lovely Christmas. We little knew what the New Year, 1935 had in store for us. Just as well or we might have trembled! In early January, David went to London for the

Board Meeting of the firm. They wanted him to take on another area, with another move for us. This was too much, we had only been at Haxby about 9 months, and David had done a lot to the garden. He resigned. It was a shock when he came home and told me.

John, Gordon and Peter 1934

Gordon, Ethel, Peter and John at Talacre 1935

Family and Wartime
1935-1945

※

    In January 1935, David started the long search for a shop to open on his own. He would be away several days, here, there and everywhere. We almost went to Loughborough, a nice new shop with flat above, very suitable, but David decided it was too far out. He wanted a busy street shop, not a little "general store". It was to be "Provisions only", a miniature "Sainsbury's". It was a worrying time; no income and knowing we must preserve the little we had to equip the shop. Eventually, he found 49 Railway Street, Altrincham. Work started on it. We had to pay cash or put down deposits as no one knew us. Somehow we managed and it was opened on

March 21st 1935.

   David found us a house in Hale, in Queens Road. We moved in February. It was hard going in many ways, 3 children and a house to buy and get in order, David was working all hours, getting things organised at the shop, buying equipment and feeling his way around the Manchester market. There was a good primary school just down the road, so the lads could come home for midday dinner and I did not have to take them and meet them etc. They settled in very well, Johnny had been very happy for the few weeks he had been at the Haxby village school so he must have found the new school rather overpowering.

   We had no car. David bought a second hand cycle and used it to take the hams we cooked at home in the evenings in bags on the front and back. It was not too far to 49 Railway Street. We had a big scullery at the house and nice kitchen, so the cooking did not bother us very much. There was a nice garden at the back, behind was a largish area, which had been a small market garden. It was sold to the builders, Tyrrell and Westlake and was being laid out for houses, a cul-de-sac, just 10 houses, 8 semi's and 2 detached at the far end. What

Gordon, Peter and John 1934

could be better? David and I watched one evening and saw several plots were already booked, but not the one we wanted, right in the corner, detached and quite a nice piece of land all around. The next morning after David had left for 49, he came back (to my surprise) and said, "It is ours! I have just put down £5 which reserves the plot." Imagine our joy, our own home at last, after 8 moves in 9 years.

Summer 1935 at York House was not easy. David was working all out at 49, and still managed to keep the garden and lawn tidy and go to Bowdon church to ring twice on Sunday. He also did the "paper" work at the office (a tiny little "box room" at the back of the shop), checked invoices, paid bills etc. We got a discount if we paid within 7 days, that was very important to us at that time – no "going in the red" for us, or anything on "instalments" either at the shop or at home.

The older boys were happy at school, and Peter very happy. He used to go round to the "plot" and talk to the workmen, they were very kind to him. He loved to see and hear the "Tut-Tut" machine (the concrete mixer). Unfortunately, Gordon got a germ and had a bad throat, and John also. Gordon got over it fairly well, but Johnny was very, very ill. We had some very anxious days. Dr Hunter was splendid, but it was a sad time for us, and such a joy when Johnny smiled and tried to speak. But he got better (bless him) and when he was well enough to be interested, I moved his bed over to the window where he could watch all that was going on and see our house being built. It was weeks before he went back to school. He was so tall and frail looking, but happy to be around. The summer and winter passed and the houses went up and up. Soon all the plots were booked and eventually we moved, in Easter 1936. We had had a very happy Christmas (1935) at York House. The boys were happy at school, they were also happy at Sunday School. This was at Hale Road Methodist Church. It was too far to the Baptist Chapel, and also a long way to the Bowdon Parish Church where David went twice on Sunday to ring.

We were very pleased with the house but the ground was very very difficult. It had been a market garden, and our little lawn had to be where all the brick structures of bedding plants had been, each walled around. It was very hard work, but by the end of the summer, the lawn had been done (by outside work, a load of turf and men to lay it down). David was buying fruit trees from Suffolk and putting up a pagola down by the narrow concrete paths as he made ready for climbing roses and ramblers.

The following year, 1937, we had a real garden. Mc-Gready roses were the thing to buy at that time and we had some of every colour and the clusters of the climbers etc were wonderful. David had said once "we will have a garden where you can pick all the flowers you need for the house and not miss them", and we did! The shop was going well. It was not so hard to get experienced and reliable staff before the 1939-45 war, otherwise David would not have been able to even look at the garden. He worked very hard at the shop, long hours, but still managed to keep a beautiful garden.

In 1938, David took over some premises in Northwich. It was a new building with offices over, and he took the shop as a shell, so there was a lot to do, floors, windows, everything. Eventually it was opened. It did well, but it was never as good as Altrincham. Northwich then was still rather rural, busy on Market day but dull other days. There were not many business people living around as there are at Hale, Bowdon and Altrincham. It is very different now. Sainsbury's now have an ugly block building and there are many other big stores. But it is really a very ugly place all told, I think, almost as bad as Stockport.

1938, also put us "back on the road." David decided that we had so little spare time to relax, and that I and the children would never go anywhere unless we went just on the "spur of the moment", when work permitted. So he went to

Ethel and boys picnicing 1937

Standard Cars at Coventry and bought a lovely little pale grey 12 HP with all the extras possible, leather, sliding roof, special windows, even three attache cases to match, which fitted into the boot. We kept it a secret from the boys. They were all three ready for bed, but I did not hurry them, hoping Daddy would arrive. It was such a lovely evening, and when this lovely little car appeared there was great excitement. We were the first people to have a car in the drive, and we were the only house with a telephone! When Daddy got out, imagine their delight! I wonder how I kept them from running out in their pyjamas but I don't think they did. It was a great joy to us.

We had a lovely holiday at Penmaenmawr (North Wales). David took us everywhere, how I loved the hills and the villages. Auntie Alice came with us, she was a widow at this time.

One day in Spring 1939, Daddy took the 3 boys to London for a day, Croydon first I believe, and then to "the sights of London". I think he (Daddy) must have had quite a busy day, one way or another. Peter insisted on buying a flower plant for me, and this had to be carried around all day. Peter also got "lost" in Selfridges, so interested in everything. But they arrived home safely, tired and happy. I expect daddy was the most "worn out".

In 1939, business was going well. Daddy booked a furnished house for a month at Whitby, Auntie Alice came to us there from Croydon. The house was very nice indeed, the boys insisted on taking Lulu the cat with us, and she behaved perfectly. One day she was out when we were going out, so we had to hope she would return. She did and was waiting for us at the gate when we returned. We had some nice picnic outings, one to Runswick Bay, a beautiful village.

David did a lot of "good ringing" while we were at Whitby, up on the hill at Whitby, Beverley, Robin Hood's Bay etc. Then Fred came to us there and when Daddy was ringing took us out by bus to different places. He was very good with the boys and it was nice to have him around to entertain them. But alas, our holiday was cut short. War was in the air. One evening David and I went for a walk along the front. Daddy pointed out away in the far distance a long line of war ships just in the fading light. We packed up the next day. Auntie and Fred went back to London by train. The station was full of evacuees from London. We left in our own car to arrive home to find the garden a mass of flowers, so beautiful.

Oh! Why did there have to be a war? It changed so much for everyone, and nothing was ever the same for us all again.

Gordon was 12 on September 2nd and started at Manchester Grammar School and was quite happy. A couple of years later, John and Peter started at Sale High School for

Boys, which was the prep school for Manchester Grammar School. Fortunately, they went safely all through the war. There were no day time air raids. The air raid sirens went at times, and the children came home early. A Saturday morning Sports Day at school came to an early end. Gordon was in the MGS Air Training Corps.

  We were very lucky in many ways during the war, only 12 miles from Manchester. Hundreds of enemy planes must have gone over us on their way to Manchester and Liverpool. But we only had two bombs dropped (on their way back we thought), one in Bradbury Central School playground near to no.6, and the other on an end cottage in Oldfield Street, a total wreck, where several people lost their lives. More or less every window was broken in Stamford Park Road and around. But we suffered no hurt, down in the half-basement-flat where we made a "home" out of two large cellars in a four storey stone house, which belonged to a lady and her niece we had become friendly with from the time we first arrived in Hale. It was the niece Mildred Wood who first took the three boys to the Methodist Sunday School.

  David was an Air Raid Warden, and the sirens seemed

David and the boys at Stanway Drive 1939

to go around tea-time each day, so he was out a lot. Auntie Alice lived with us a lot during the war. She was "bombed out" at Croydon, and later they had "doodle-bugs" at Beckenham. The children and I would leave number 6 and go down to the "cellar flat". We took beds and everything we needed and were very comfortable. Water and gas were laid on, and David had the whole place white-washed. Our entrance was down steps at the side of the house, and we often had several other families with children plus people there with us who were nervous of being alone. With the planes overhead I was never short of tea. Being six of us we had always a cup to spare if required. Nicky, our lovely black cat, was always with us. Sometimes he crept out and David often felt him rubbing around his legs if he was anywhere near us. David was also "Red Cross", and passed his second "grade" during this time.

We were not far from Ringway, the Airport. It was then open fields where hundreds of men and women worked on planes damaged during their raids over Germany. The Services took over men employees, and the Munitions works took away the girls who followed the men as assistants in the shop. We had no girl labour before the war. Northwich shop was closed. We could not staff it, but we were fortunate to be able to let it to the government for ration book services.

It was a blessing that I was able to cope with all the paperwork, ration cards and coupons. Even the boys sometimes helped, all of us together round the dining room table, sorting out different colour coupons, which had to be used for our "perishable" goods. It was a lot of work for a few ounces of food, but very precious for us to obtain supplies.

Our garden was very beautiful at this time, the result of four years work and care. There were roses of every colour.

Peter, John and Gordon 1939

I wish I had some coloured snaps of it, but films just disappeared from the shops with many other things we had been used to. We had apples, pears, and cherry trees. We were never short of fruit, and the greenhouse produced tomatoes and cucumbers. David had an allotment. Several wardens took over some land near Altrincham football ground which was quite near. Each had a plot and enjoyed the competition against each other. We also had a few hens, so there were eggs for use, fed almost entirely by cooking vegetable peelings, but we were allowed a small ration of corn on permit.

Petrol was rationed and was only available for business and professions, and could only be used over a limited distance. But in 1943 we managed to rent a Chalet at Tynymorfa, North Wales, I took Auntie and Fred there with the boys. David and I joined them at weekends and took their rations, vegetables etc.

Gordon had left Manchester Grammar School and was doing a year's practical farming with a farmer in Dunham. This was compulsory to ensure a place for him at Reaseheath, Nantwich, Agricultural College. In his year there, 1944-1945 he did very well and came out second of all the students. He met Betty Skellern there, she was in the Dairy group and also did very well. Only one year was allowed, so they could not go further for a degree, neither could they have gone to any other college outside Cheshire. Gordon and Betty married on Christmas Day, 1948.

Ethel and Betty 1947

Ethel and David 1950

Completing the Story

※

The Provision Specialist
Peter Vincent

David Vincent had worked for John Sainsbury from April 1913, volunteering and serving in the Middlesex Regiment for over four years between 1914 and 1918. After the war he returned to the company and worked in and around the Croydon area. He progressed quickly to branch manager. One of his first appointments was as relief manager at the Tunbridge Wells branch, where he met and later married the Head Book-keeper, Ethel Beatrice Gadd. They moved to several other locations until David was invited to take on the role of District Inspector with a Northern based firm called Thoroughgoods.

1934 saw the closure of most of the North Eastern branches, and in spite of an invitation to join a reformed company, David decided that it was time to go it alone. In March 1935 he opened his first specialist provision shop at 49 Railway Street, Altrincham. No one had ever seen a shop like it and it was an instant success.

In 1938 David opened his second branch at Witton Street, Northwich. Always finding time from her busy family commitments, Ethel kept all the book-keeping up to date, leaving David to run the practical side.

The war meant hard and frustrating times of food rationing, which lasted until the mid 1950's. Regulations stated that retailers could only have a permit to sell goods they had previously sold, and this for a specialist business such as theirs hit very hard.

David once more volunteered for military service, but was turned down on the grounds that as a public food distributor he was in a reserved occupation. The company and the family somehow survived, and money was always found for a good education for the boys. Gordon studied agriculture

David Vincent Manager in the 1920's

and John did National Service and then became a Methodist Minister. It was the youngest son Peter who entered the business when he left school at 16 in 1949. Ethel worked behind the counter as well in those days, and slipped away to the little office at the back to put up the wages and pay the bills. When Peter returned from National Service in 1953, the Altrincham shop was back to pre-war conditions, and was once more very successful.

Peter married in 1956, and with two families to feed, a programme of expansion was started. The first branch was at King Street in Stretford, quickly followed by School Road, Sale.

Number 125 Northenden Road, Sale Moor was the next branch, where the premises were large enough to accommodate not only the offices for the now fast growing David Vincent Ltd, but also space for the development of a cooked meat and sausage manufacturing plant, bacon processing and packaging, and later a bakery for pies and pastries. For several years Ethel, now in her 70's used to make the journey from their home in High Leigh every Thursday to Sale Moor, to help with the running of the office and the book-keeping. Altrincham now had two branches, the second in George Street, and further shops were opened in Macclesfield, Wilmslow, Urmston and Timperley.

With David's help and encouragement, eldest son Gordon started farming on his own in 1950 at Charlesworth, Derbyshire. Later Gordon specialised in poultry and egg production, and formed Honey Brown Farm Eggs Ltd. This

David as Grand Master, Sale 1945

became the sole supplier to all the David Vincent shops until 1992.

    Although David and Ethel did celebrate their 50th Wedding Anniversary together in 1975, David died on 15th July 1976. It was left to Ethel to head the table some ten years later at the 50th Anniversary of the company in March 1985. She was presented with the "Wait for me" painting that hung in her bedroom and now hangs in Peter's house. It was perhaps a little ironic that in that year Sainsbury's, the company where David and Ethel had first met, should open their first northern Supermarket in Altrincham.

Although some of the branches continued to trade well, the pattern of the culture was beginning to become clear. The expansion of the Supermarkets and out of town shopping precincts, the general decline of the main streets, and the change of people's shopping habits plus parking restrictions all began to take their toll. It was fortunate that there was not another generation hoping to take over the company, so over the next few years the company quietly closed its branches one by one. The last branch to close was the first branch that David had opened at 49 Railway Street, Altrincham. It was almost 57 years to the day, in June 1992.

David was always known and referred to as 'The Governor.' His philosophy was simple. Try to make people feel hungry and never sell anything that you would not buy and eat yourself.

I add some words spoken at Mothers Funeral:

David Vincent shops Golden Anniversary 1985

    I thought that I was handling this situation quite well until last Saturday when a pianist at a wedding played an old song titled "When I grow too old to dream" that goes on "I'll have you to remember." Mother re-wrote the words into a lullaby and used to sing it to us. It ended "when you grow too tired to play, you'll creep into your mummy's arms." Then everything fell to pieces.

    When my brother John was a senior prefect at Manchester Grammar School he had to take his turn to select and read the lessons at morning prayers for a week and mother and I used to listen to him rehearsing at home. One of the lessons was from the first letter of Paul to the Corinthians that ended in the old translation with "and now abideth faith, hope and charity." It was one of her favourite readings. I remember saying that 'charity' as we knew it then was an unusual thing to be so important, and it was mother who told us that it was about kindness and sharing and thinking about others and about love. All this was in the mid forties and long before the New English Bible re-wrote the verse into "there are three things that last forever, faith, hope and love, but the greatest of them all is love."

Well, there is no doubt that mother had her 'faith' which she kept to the end. She never lost hope, not just for herself but for her family, her friends, her church, her country and her world. And she was never ever short of love.

In 1985, browsing round a picture gallery in Altrincham, mother suddenly grasped my wife's arm and said "wait for me." As they were together, Margaret was somewhat bemused until mother explained that it was a picture showing a little Victorian girl who had stopped to tie her shoe laces and

Ethel Vincent on her 108th birthday

was calling to two boys who were busy walking on looking at some fish in a jam jar. It appears that the same picture was in the guesthouse when mother and her sister May had gone on their first holiday with their mother and father in 1897 when she was just six years old. She had never seen it again until that day. We gave mother the picture when we celebrated the 50 year anniversary of the business that she and father had started in Altrincham in 1935. It has always had pride of place in her room since then.

The waiting is over, our little Victorian girl need wait no longer.

*Gordon and John in the garden at
'Sunnyside" Prestatyn 1933*

Childhood and Family Life
Gordon Vincent

✂

My early memories were somewhat confused by the ever changing locations we lived in, due to father being moved from shop to shop by his firm (Thoroughgoods).

One to stand out in 1932, was the holiday in Tynymorfa, near Prestatyn. Mother organised John and myself, in a self help chalet at the edge of the sand dunes there. The chalet, was to say the least, very basic, but mother had the place spick and span by the end of the holiday, which was a very happy one for her, I am sure.

Grandma Gadd died in 1934, and it had a lasting effect on Mother, they had been very close. Mother talked to us about Grandma and life at home prior to getting married. Parts of this period of her life she sadly missed at times.

The next really momentous decision, business apart, had been the purchase in 1935 of the plot which became No 6 Stanway Drive, mother's first real home, she called it. Here she could plan ahead, and quietly get the things she wanted in it from father. Eight moves to different houses, in far flung situations, since her marriage in 1926 had left its mark, and she was very determined that this new house was to be a permanent dwelling. Father, who had had no permanent home since before 1914, had no doubt got used to lodgings and rented accommodation; and possibly did not share mother's enthusiasm.

The shop at 49 Railway Street, Altrincham prospered so one day father appeared at our house with a spanking new car, a state of the art streamlined "Flying Standard 12" made by the Standard Motor Company in Coventry in 1938. Mother

The "lovely sleek grey car", the Flying Standard

was over the moon, there was a car to house her family as she thought there should be, and she took great delight in organising outings in this "lovely sleek grey car," as she liked to describe it.

My parents had not had a car since shortly after John was born, and father had been cycling or bussing to work since the family had moved to Hale. The bike which had trade plates on it, had doubled up for deliveries. I had to use it sometimes for Dad's deliveries to favoured customers. It was never made for a 10-year old to pedal, to be sure.

Mother took over all the book-keeping for the business including the new shop opened in Northwich in 1938. She no doubt dropped hints about help, in the form of a maid, to Father. These hints fell on terrible ground! Father had the builders, who had built our house, to build a fourth bedroom over the kitchen/scullery. Father had thought was for book-keeping. Next we knew, Mother had a maid named Betty, installed in the new room. She was well educated, from a good home, and we three children took to her like a second mum, and mother encouraged Betty to take John and myself, who were old enough, out pleasure trips. These included picture going, shows, Bring and Buys, Belle Vue, and even 'speedway' and the infamous 'Bobs' at Belle Vue (an ageing "Helter Skelter")

These outings, kept partially secret from father in case they were frowned upon, were meant by Mother to broaden her 'boys' outlooks prior to 1940.

The pinnacle of Mother's week, now she had a maid, was organising Sunday Lunch in the dining room. Always three courses, the best silver – yes, silver that had to be cleaned in those days, was laid out, in front of her boys, who had been washed and in their "Sunday Best" ready for departure at 2.15pm prompt to Sunday School. This was a mammoth task, getting this to her high standards. We had probably been helping father in the morning in our "roughs", anything from gardening to recreosoting pagodas. In our hectic lifestyle today, all this may appear very pedestrian, but to mother, the home and the way it was run was of prime importance, just as father judged success in business terms.

War broke out with Germany in September 1939 and Mother told us boys that it would affect us all before long. It was hard to believe at first that we were at war, but after a while Mother's prediction proved correct. Father lost two key staff to the Army by the spring of 1940. Two more men followed that summer, and mother lost her maid and companion Betty, who joined the A.T.S.

A new Resident maid called Kathleen, Irish from Westport, joined the family, allowing Mother to spend more time at the shop helping father, who by this time had been forced to shut the Northwich branch shop. Kathleen and mother got on particularly well. Kathleen admired mother's organising skills, and mother found someone she could trust and confide in with confidence. Mother appeared to miss female company with which she could discuss quietly the day to day running of the home, as father was never interested. It could have been the same with Betty, our previous maid, but I was too young to notice.

Father's lifelong hobby, Church bell change ringing was hit hard when a ban was introduced on Church bells ringing aloud except for times of invasion. The family therefore set about learning the art of change hand bell ringing, and we rang change courses at many church, chapel and social events during the war. Hand bell ringing was important to mother, not that she liked it particularly, but it gave her a chance to present her family as one unit, very essential in her eyes.

Organising the family, including Father, in their "Sunday Best" for these events, presented a challenge to mother,

Ethel and the boys 1936

which she relished at the time. If the ringing had been "change perfect" at the event, this was an added bonus to her, as father glowed with pride and satisfaction after a good event. The average listener at the functions applauded, not knowing the "grade difficulty" of each particular change. But to father perfection in striking and changes was of prime importance, so we spent many wartime evenings practising, between homework and other duties.

Alice, dad's eldest sister, bombed out early in the war

in Croydon, London, lived with us at times at no 6. She had a broad sense of humour and acted as a lighthearted peacemaker, coming to mother's aid in no uncertain fashion at critical times of family strife. Dad held Alice in some awe, probably because she had brought him up after his mother had died.

Our maid Kathleen, who was courting at night would be coming in around the same time as father and would act as a very capable Irish peacemaker when father returned from the United Services or Altrincham football club, the worse for drink, providing lighter humour at critical times. She no doubt had plenty of experience of similar situations back in Ireland, "hear all, lay it low and tomorrow it had never happened."

As the war progressed, lack of turnover due to increased rationing meant a gradually reducing income for the household. Mother, handling the accounts knew better than anyone, and she turned to helping father at times behind the counter as well as handling all the coupon side of rationing, a most tedious product. Father got very depressed at times. All his shop labour was now female, and he had no knowledge from past experience to guide him when dealing with the fairer sex.

Mother tried to make clothes last longer, a difficult feat with three fast growing sons. My own toes bear the results of shoes being repaired too often. Peter started school terms with John's clothes and upwards. Mother encouraged me to cycle to Manchester Grammar School when the weather was decent, and I was given part of the train fare as pocket money.

An allotment was taken over, near Altrincham Football Club, and mother encouraged all the boys to help father work at it. She presided over the arguments about whose turn it was, so as to give father the impression we were all willing helpers.

We kept hens for egg laying in several pens outside the kitchen window. I also kept rabbits for breeding and showing, though most of the rabbits did not win and ended up in stews or pies. The main mourner when they eventually arrived on the table was father, who had got quite attached to the odd rabbit or two, and particularly liked bringing discarded "greens" from the allotment and feeding both rabbits and hens himself. Mother encouraged John and myself to take rabbits we bred to shows, with which, to our surprise, some success was gained. We took them on the bus or cycled with them in baskets, but we had our innocent eyes opened at these shows. I suppose we thought everyone was honest. Mother persuaded father to bring her to one of these shows, and proudly photographed our prizewinners outside the show entrances.

In 1943 I got my school certificate at 15. I left and mother got me a place on Home Farm, Dunham Massey, for 12 months prior to going to Reaseheath for a year's course in General Agriculture. As I knew father was short of money, I proudly presented mother with half my wages every week – this amounted to the princely sum of 15 shillings; not enough I learned later.

Mother was worried over home bills in 1944, and to keep John and Peter at Manchester Grammar School, father cashed in one of his Hearts of Oak 'Benefits' he had paid into since 1913. Mother confided this to me a little later but it was not until I was much older that I realised what a blow this had been to my parents. It was equivalent to cashing in one

Boys at Stanway Drive 1943

person's pension today at the age of 48. I felt some guilt that I was not helping father in his business, and told my parents that I would delay going to Reaseheath School of Agriculture, and carry on working as a breadwinner for a further year, as I was now working weekends and earning more which I handed over to mother. They considered this option but in September 1944, I learned that I had been granted a full board and fees scholarship for a year's course at Reaseheath College of Agriculture. Father insisted I take it, pointing out that I was now just 17 and in 12 months time or later would be eligible for a call up, and the place might disappear for me at College. So mother backed father, perhaps reluctantly, as she would miss her long talks with me about life at Tunbridge prior to 1914. Her memory of her childhood, teenage and young adult days was very vivid and one gathered that in spite of financial difficulties at home, her upbringing had been a very happy one.

My teenage memories of mother and life at home finish here, as I left home in 1944 not to return except for a short spell, at father's request, when mother was ill in 1948. As a postscript, I must mention the financial support my family had from Mother and Father, when I commenced farming in 1953. Without it, Woodseats Farm, Charlesworth, Derbyshire would have been a nonstarter for us. Luckily when Father needed the money, we were able to refinance his loans and repay him some years after.

David Vincent 1950\s

David and Ethel outside their two berth caravan 1950's

Later Years
By John Vincent

※

A new chapter began for mother in 1976 when David died. I preface a few memories of those last few years by recording some details about father.

On holiday with father and mother, in the 1940's, I went with father and visited a small derelict cottage in the middle of a field in Fressingfield, Suffolk. It had two bedrooms and in one of them I picked up two old books. Dad encouraged me to take them as they had been theirs. Dad had been born on November 21st 1897 in this cottage, from where he had walked to Stradbroke to school, 5 miles away.

There were 11 children in all who all lived in this tiny cottage, amongst whom can be named, Alice, John (died as a child), Lottie (who went to Australia), Frank (who lived at Beckenham), Fred (who was gassed in the war), Charlie (who died at the siege of Knut) and Jim (who died at Hill aged 20).

Dad's mother died around 1910, and as a young teenager with his father went to live with Alice (eldest child) at Campsie Ashe. David remained there to finish school where he spent the last years as a pupil teacher/monitor. Alice's daughter Vi was a younger contemporary of David. On leaving school he went into gentleman's service and then started with J Sainsbury's on the 4th of April 1913. As soon as he was old enough he joined up in November 1914, at 18 years of age, and served in the Middlesex Regiment, going to France at 19 (not being allowed to go until then).

The experience of being a sniper in the trenches for two years created a traumatic memory for dad. He would sometimes be quite overcome by memories "You cannot have any idea of it Johnny, can you?" he would say. He had several books on the war in his bookcase, including All Quiet on the Western Front, and he went to France for a reunion and a

Ethel and dog Flu Flutouring in the 50's

memorial gathering in 1958.

    Mother and father moved away to Mere Hayes in 1960 and then in 1968 to 8, Deanway in Wilmslow. After father died in 1976, mother spent intermittent periods with all three sons, but went back to their home in Wilmslow, until 1979. Then, after six months in Charlesworth at Woodseats Farm with Gordon and Betty, she moved to a flat at 233 Abbeyfield Road, and from there to a room with John and Grace at 239 Abbeyfield Road Sheffield in 1981. She moved with them to 178 Abbeyfield Road, in July 1991. For as long as she was able, and certainly up to her 100th year, mother continued to go for holiday breaks to stay with Gordon and Peter. Often one of them took her away with them on their holidays – as of course did Grace and myself and our three children.

For quite a long time, from 1986 to 2000, our home was a continuation of the family home that mother had created for us in our childhood. It was a time of quite special richness for us – and a time when all the children, grandchildren and great grandchildren would come and visit "Bamma", as she had come to be called. Christmas and New Year were especially crowded, as was the memorable 100th Birthday day at 239. Mother's birthday was 8th January.

It is worth recalling that until her marriage at 36, mother had little experience of children, and none of boys. So she used memories of her own childhood as a guide. She would call for us after Sunday School, and take us for a walk in Hale Barns, a bus ride away. Her own recollections of her 'hurts' as a child with glasses made her sensitive to any child's hurts - ours or anyone else's. Her glory in sunsets lasted till the end.

Mere Hayes Christmas 1964

"Come up and look at the sunset", she would call. And the gardens and flowers she grew up with, she and dad created for us, too.

    Mother remained alert and active to the end. She greatly valued the seasons. "Another Spring, Johnny", she would say. Or, on her birthday, "I don't know what I'm doing, still here. I think God has forgotten me!" In fact, she believed that God had very much not forgotten her – or anyone else, for that matter.

A friend Beryl Peck, once asked whether mother would be prepared to be interviewed by a social science researcher who was investigating the deterioration of memory in older people. The researcher duly arrived with her 100 questions. Grace asked whether she could do the questions as well, so they both sat writing their answers. At the end, mother's total score was 92, whereas Grace's was only 78. Mother's comment in excusing Grace's performance was, "Well, she's not as old as I am, is she?" Which was exactly the opposite of what the researcher was trying to illustrate!

Grace and I frequently had people say to us that it must have been a burden to have mother with us – and did we not need a break? We had to reply, in all honesty, that mother was not a burden, but was simply a vital part of our family. Our children and grandchildren were constantly with her up in her room, and she greatly enjoyed their company and the games they played.

In the last 18 months, mother was confined upstairs, mainly in her own room, and Grace or I had to be at home at all times. My two brothers came over for short periods when

Ethel Vincent in 1976

Grace and I had to be away. Mother lived with us at home up to the last 7 weeks of her life, when we had to move her into the St. Catherine's Home at the end of our road.

In the last few weeks of mother's life, only two sets of words came from her. Up until her stroke on 6th March, and her move to St Catherine's home on 9th March, she had still been able to communicate on all manner of things. But in the last few weeks only two elements came to her faltering and slow speech. And they indicate what was significant for her

– what was in her mind, if not always her consciousness.

First, it was the names and memories of her family. Peter had come over on April 17th, his birthday, and I told her of this the next day. "Johnny, that's terrible," she said. "I had forgotten it was his birthday." I said that she could not be expected to remember all the birthdays any more. But right up till then, she remembered all the 47 birthdays of every one of the sons, daughters in law, grandchildren, great grand children and (by then) one great great grand child. Mother's life had been spent on us. We were the centre and soul of her concern. So that mother's life, above all, has its significance in her model of total commitment to the support and care of those who belonged to her, and to whom she belonged. And, for myself, to be able to minister a bit to her in her helplessness towards the end, was a logical and proper way of returning services to her that she had ministered to me at the very beginning of my own life, as a tiny child.

The other word on her mind and on her lips were the words of her faith in God. At the end of my visits, she would say, "Say a Prayer," and I said it slowly, as she would follow

Vincent family at Wake at 178 in 2000

and join in every word. When I took communions with her, she would say every word of the service with me. The prayers which we said at the funeral were particular favourites with her – they were part of her being, and were the source to which she turned. It was part of her that was there, even when consciousness was fading.

One other thing of significance for us:

Mother had great problem with people who did evil or wrong things. Basically, she could not believe that anyone would do evil. When anything wrong occurred, or someone failed at something, she would immediately put a good gloss on it. She simply did not believe that it was possible to intend evil. I have never heard her say an ill word about anyone. That ultimate faith in people, faith in goodness, and determination, to speak only of the good, was to me a powerful force.

So, mum had made it into her third century! And into the lives of us all she leaves indelible and dear memories, and an act hard to follow. As Faith wrote recently, "You had a fabulous, strong, courageous mother." And all of us in the extended family are heirs to that inheritance, and bits of it are hopefully in our genes and remain there as our children's children and their children read and treasure and perhaps even live by pieces of these memories.

Ethel at 239 Abbeyfield Road in 1992

from left to right:
David with Gordon 1929; David, Gordon and Ethel at Tonbridge in July 1930; David Vincent 1918

from left to right:
Gordon and his pram; Ethel, John and Gordon taken at Tonbridge, July 1930; Ethel ad Gordon 1928

119